W9-CAG-670

BOOKS BY SCOTT CORBETT

The Trick Books

THE LEMONADE TRICK
THE MAILBOX TRICK
THE DISAPPEARING DOG TRICK
THE LIMERICK TRICK
THE BASEBALL TRICK
THE TURNABOUT TRICK
THE HAIRY HORROR TRICK

What Makes It Work?

WHAT MAKES A CAR GO?
WHAT MAKES TV WORK?
WHAT MAKES A LIGHT GO ON?
WHAT MAKES A PLANE FLY?
WHAT MAKES A BOAT FLOAT?

Suspense Stories

MIDSHIPMAN CRUISE
TREE HOUSE ISLAND
DEAD MAN'S LIGHT
CUTLASS ISLAND
DANGER POINT: THE WRECK OF THE BIRKENHEAD
ONE BY SEA
THE CASE OF THE GONE GOOSE
COP'S KID
THE CASE OF THE FUGITIVE FIREBUG
THE BASEBALL BARGAIN

What Makes a Boat Float?

What Makes a

BOAT FLOAT?

by Scott Corbett

Pictures by Victor Mays

An Atlantic Monthly Press Book

LITTLE, BROWN AND COMPANY

BOSTON TORONTO

LIBRARY OF CONGRESS CATALOG CARD NO. 76-94498

FIRST EDITION

ATLANTIC-LITTLE, BROWN BOOKS
ARE PUBLISHED BY
LITTLE, BROWN AND COMPANY
IN ASSOCIATION WITH
THE ATLANTIC MONTHLY PRESS

Published simultaneously in Canada
by Little, Brown & Company (Canada) Limited

PRINTED IN THE UNITED STATES OF AMERICA

To Bob Flandreau

What makes a boat float?

Buoyancy.

What is buoyancy?

To understand buoyancy, we must use two kinds of measurement: volume and weight.

The amount of space that any object takes up is called its volume.

The quantity of matter in an object is called its mass, and the pull of gravity on an object's mass is what we call its weight.

Water is heavy. If we had a container one foot long, one foot wide, and one foot high, its volume would be one cubic foot. A container this size does not seem large, yet if we filled it with fresh water the water would weigh about 62.4 pounds. If we filled it with salt water from the ocean, the water would weigh about 64 pounds.

When an object is placed in water, its weight causes it to push down against the water. The object sinks in, pushing some water out of the way and taking its place. This effect is called displacement.

A Greek mathematician born at Syracuse in Sicily in 287 B.C. discovered how displacement works. His name was Archimedes. A golden crown had been made for the king of Syracuse, but the king doubted that it was made of pure gold. He suspected that some silver had been mixed in with the gold. He asked Archimedes to find a way to prove whether he was right. At first Archimedes was puzzled. Then one day when he stepped into his bath and saw how the water level rose in the tub, he knew how to solve the problem.

Gold weighs more than silver. It has greater density. The more mass an object has in proportion to its volume, the more dense it is said to be. In other words, a pound of gold takes up less space than a pound of silver.

An amount of pure gold equal in weight to the crown could be placed in a bowl of water, and the amount of water it displaced could be measured. The same thing could be done with the crown. If the crown displaced more water than the gold, it would mean that the crown's volume was greater, and therefore it was not pure gold.

When he thought of this, Archimedes was so excited that he leaped out of his bathtub and ran naked through the streets shouting "Eureka!"—which means "I have found it!"

The law he worked out is this: A body partially or completely immersed in a fluid is

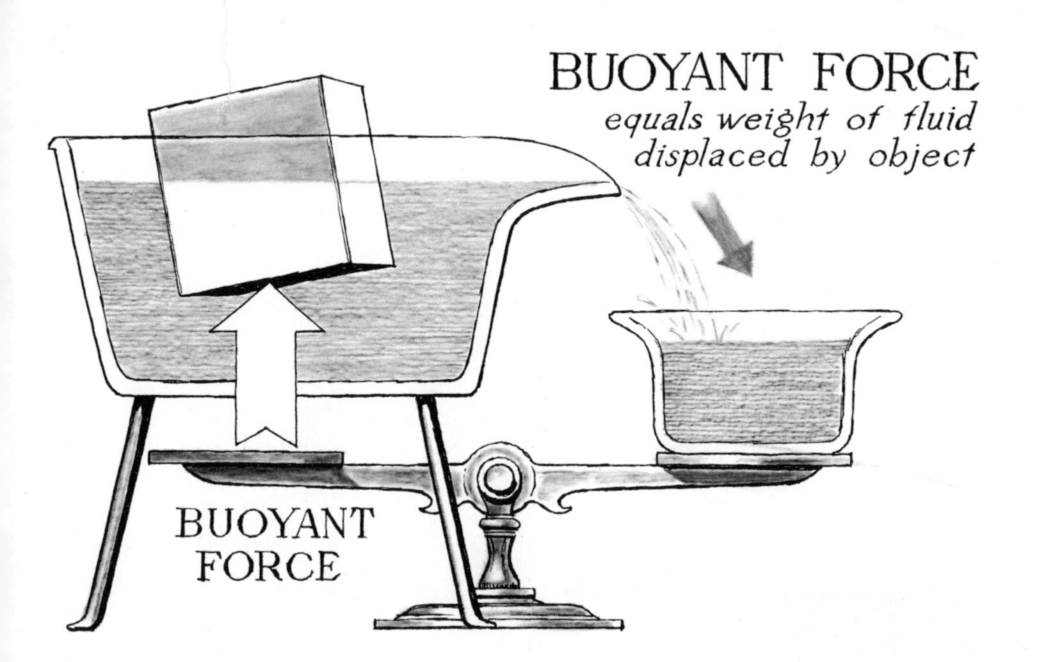

buoyed up by a force equal to the weight of the fluid it displaces.

If an object's density is greater than that of an equal volume of water, it sinks. If it is less dense, it floats. For example, a cubic foot of pine wood may weigh 32 pounds. This is half as much as the 64 pounds a cubic foot of salt water weighs. Therefore only half of the wood will sink into the water, and half will stay above it.

The relationship between these weights is called the wood's specific gravity. In this case, since it weighs only half as much as water, its specific gravity would be 0.5. Gold, on the other hand, has a specific gravity of 19, because it weighs 19 times as much as water.

It is easy, then, to see why a boat made of wood will float. But what about boats such as ocean liners and warships and freighters, which are made of steel?

Steel is much heavier than water. Its specific gravity is 7.85. A cubic foot of steel weighs 490 pounds. Placed in water, it would of course sink to the bottom.

But suppose we hollow out the steel cube, leaving only thin plates of steel on the bottom and sides of the cube. Now most of its weight has been taken away, but the cube's volume remains the same.

If the sides are now one-eighth of an inch thick, the steel cube weighs about 25 pounds. The cubic foot of air inside it weighs about three-quarters of a pound. The hollow cube weighs much less than an equal volume of water. Now it will float.

The body of a boat is called her hull.

Hulls have frames and beams inside them for support. Some frames and beams stretch from port to starboard (crosswise) and some from stem to stern (lengthwise). Port is the left side and starboard the right side of a boat, facing forwards. The stem is the forward part, the stern is the aft part.

Everything that is added to a boat increases her weight and makes her displace more water. She rides lower in the water.

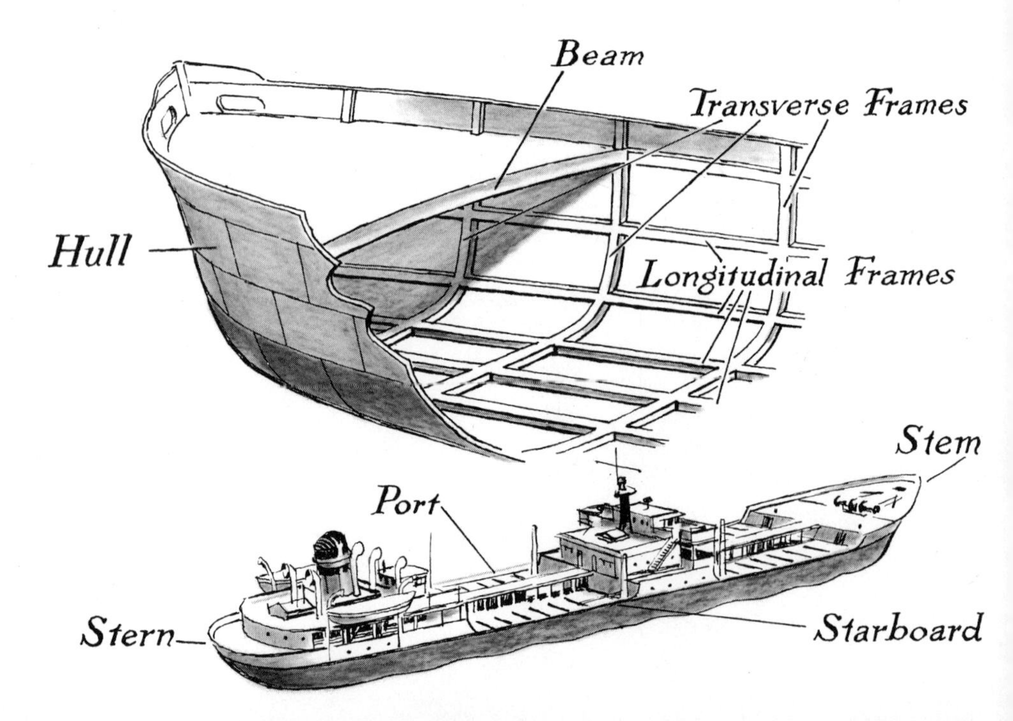

If a man gets into a boat, his weight makes the hull displace still more water and ride still lower. When the boat is a small one, we easily see how much difference the added weight makes.

The part of the outside of a boat's hull that is just at the water level is called her waterline. As extra weight is added, this line rises higher and higher.

When too many people get in, the weight of the boat becomes more than the total weight of water she can displace. The boat is pushed below the surface.

If the boat is made of wood, she will float to the surface as soon as she is free of the added weight. But if she comes to the surface right side up, she will be full of water, and its weight will prevent her from rising very much above the surface.

If she is made of steel the boat will not rise back to the surface when she is freed of additional weight. Once she is under water, her steel plates will displace only their own volume of water, and since they are heavier than water, she will sink to the bottom.

The part of a boat's hull that stays above the water is called her freeboard. On small open boats, such as rowboats, this is the space between the gunwales and the waterline. A gunwale is the upper edge of a boat's or ship's sides.

Large oceangoing boats are usually called ships. A ship's freeboard is the space between the uppermost watertight deck and the waterline.

The part of the hull that is under water gives the ship buoyancy. The watertight part between the deck and the waterline gives her an extra amount of buoyancy. This is called her reserve buoyancy.

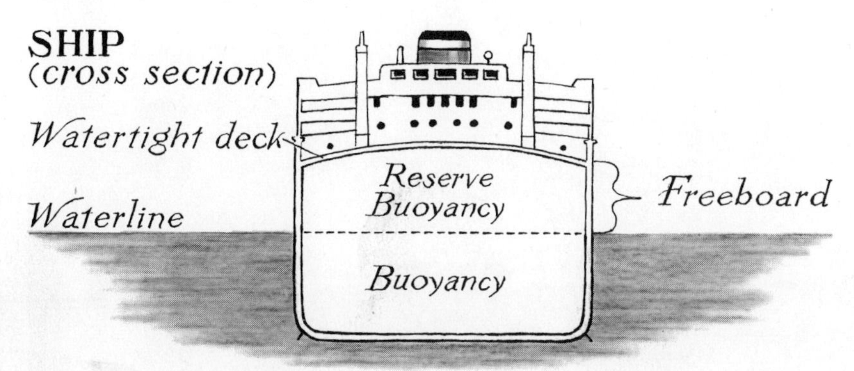

Freeboard and reserve buoyancy are important to a ship's safety. It is the reserve buoyancy that permits a ship to carry more weight than normal, and prevents sinking if she should become partially flooded.

If there were no wind and waves to make a boat roll from side to side, freeboard and reserve buoyancy would not be as important as they are. But when wind and waves make a boat roll, she needs enough freeboard to keep water from coming inside.

When she has a watertight deck to give her reserve buoyancy, then even if water comes over the side she will be safe, because it will not flow into her hull. It will run off the deck back into the sea through the scuppers, which are drains at the edge of the deck. Decks slope down slightly from the center to the sides to make it easier for water to run off. This rounded effect is called camber.

The rise of a boat's deck fore and aft is called her sheer. The rise gives her more freeboard along her bow and her stern than she has amidships, and this helps to keep water from flooding over the bow or stern.

TUG

When waves make a boat roll in one direction, why doesn't she keep going in that direction and capsize? Why does she roll back again?

To understand this, we must first understand something called the boat's stability.

Stability is the capacity of an object to return to its original position when displaced by an outside force. For a boat, stability is a relationship between her center of gravity and her center of buoyancy.

What is a center of gravity?

An object's center of gravity is the point from which its weight is evenly distributed in all directions. Any object that has weight has a center of gravity.

When a seesaw is level, with equal weight on each end, its center of gravity is exactly over its center support. All of its weight presses straight down at that point.

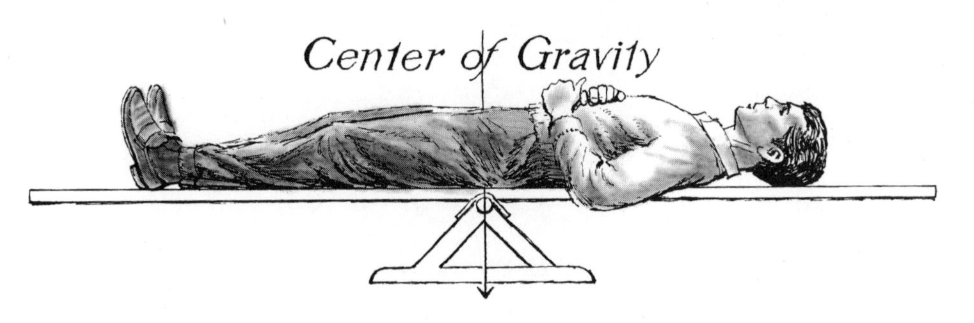

Suppose you lie flat on the center of a seesaw, with your head and shoulders on one side and your hips and legs on the other. When the seesaw is exactly level, your center of gravity is directly over the center support. Half of your weight is on one side and half on the other, and the total amount of your weight is balanced directly over the center support.

A boat in water also has a center of gravity, a point at which her weight is exactly balanced. Half of her weight is above this point, and half is below. Half is to port and half to starboard. Half is forward of this point, and half is aft. The entire weight of the boat is pressing down on the water at her center of gravity.

What is a boat's center of buoyancy?

A boat's center of buoyancy is a point from which all her buoyancy is pressing straight up with a force equal and opposite to the force pressing down from the center of gravity.

The center of buoyancy is located where the center of gravity of the displaced water would be if the water were inside the boat's hull. Since the water has been displaced, the pressure at this point is upward instead of downward.

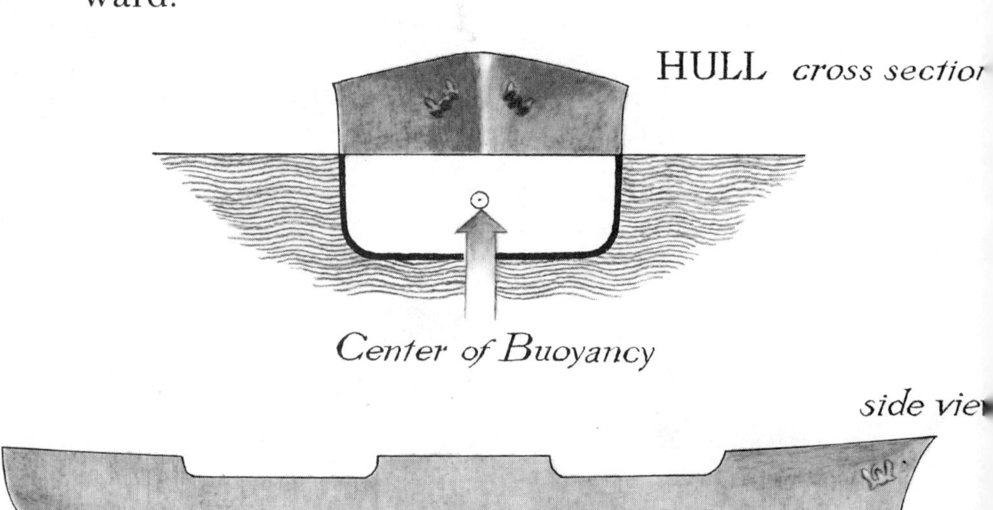

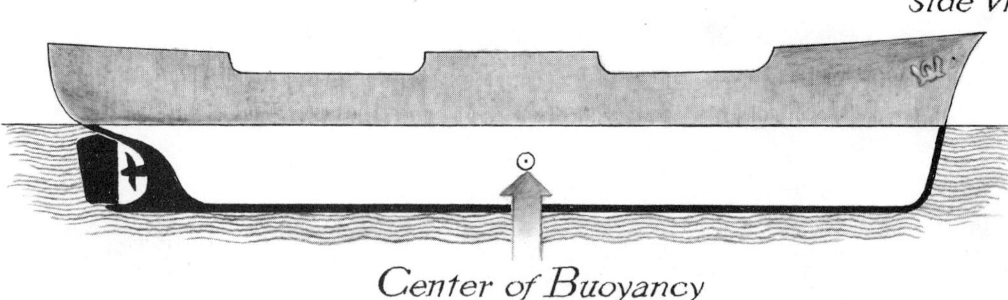

The upward pressure at the center of buoyancy is equal to the downward pressure at the center of gravity, because the weight of the water displaced is equal to the weight of the boat.

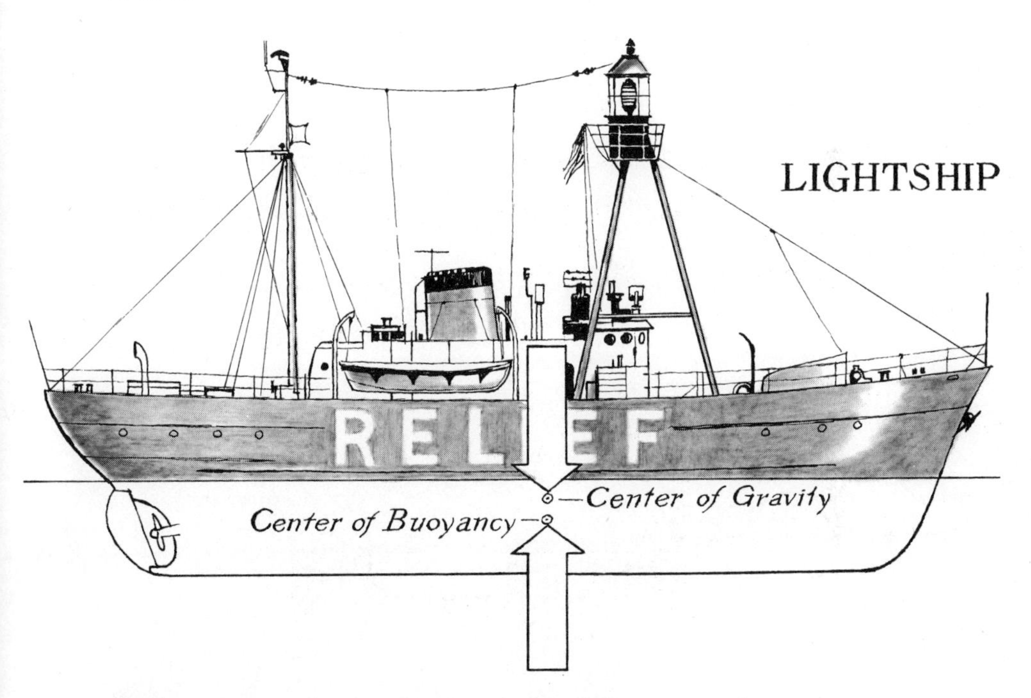

When a boat is in equilibrium, her center of buoyancy is directly under her center of gravity.

Hold a book in front of you against the edge of a table, with an inch or two of the book sticking up above the tabletop. The book is the stern of our boat, and the edge of the table is our waterline.

Now let's pretend that a wave makes our boat tip down on the starboard side.

When the boat tips, her center of gravity stays in its place on the center line. The boat rotates around the center of gravity. But the center of buoyancy stays where it was. When the boat tips, then, the center of buoyancy moves sideways, as far as the boat is concerned.

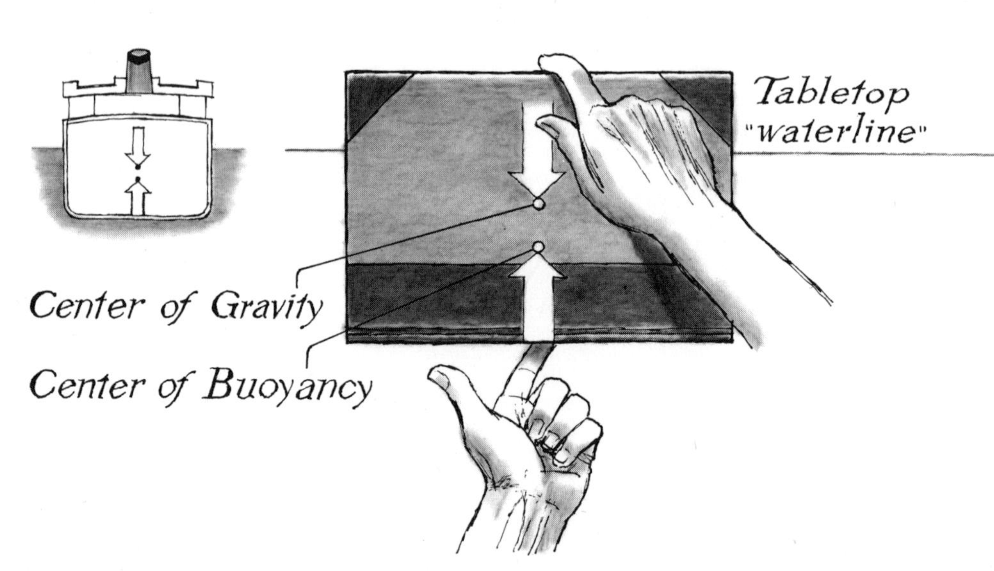

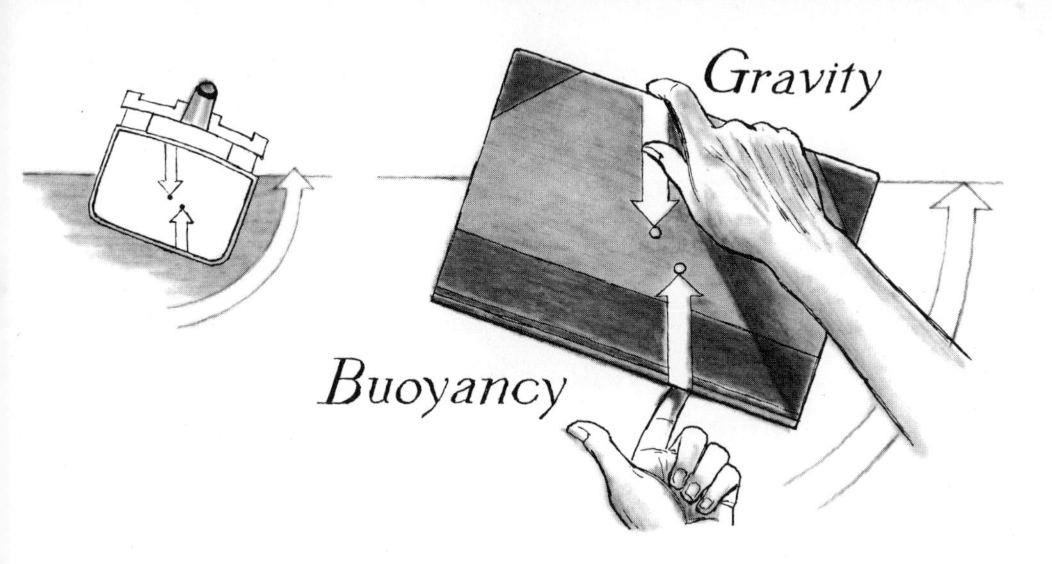

Now the center of buoyancy is no longer pressing upward in the same line as the center of gravity is pressing downward. The two forces are still parallel, and still at right angles to the waterline, but now they are no longer directly opposed to each other.

Hold the tipped book at the two points where the lines of force are shown. Push down for gravity, and up for buoyancy.

The book tips up again.

The opposing forces, gravity and buoyancy, resist the tipping motion and push the boat upright again.

But next let's assume we have added a lot of weight to the deck of our boat. When we add weight on top, we raise the center of gravity. And now, if we tip our book, this is what happens to our lines of force. They have changed positions.

Press down and up in the places shown by the new lines of force, and see what happens.

The book continues to tip over.

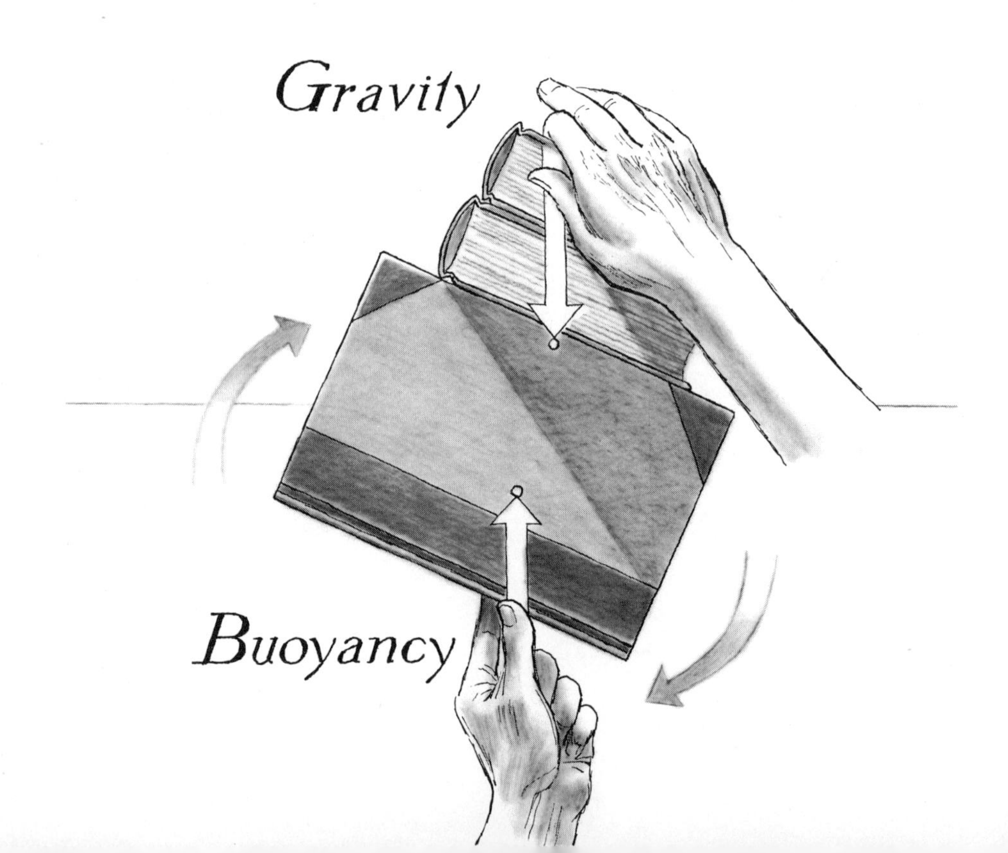

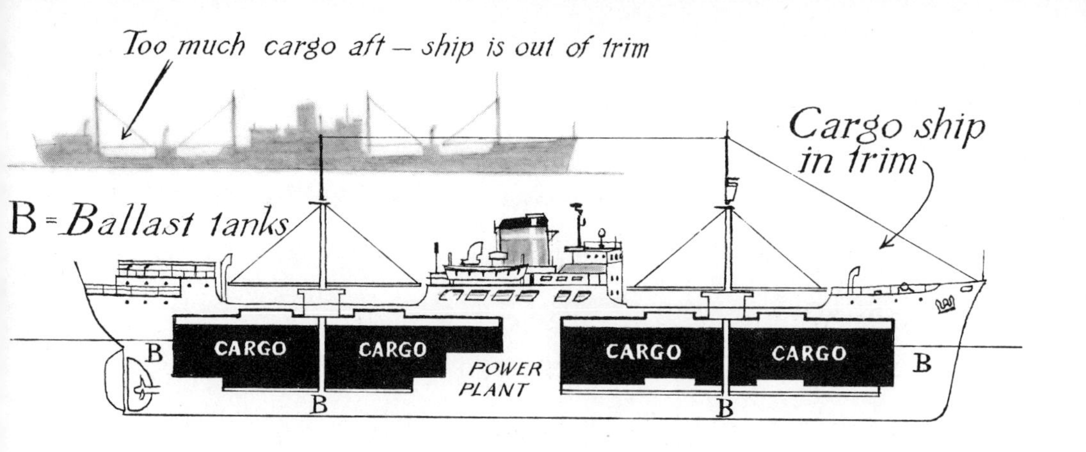

When a ship is loaded with cargo, the cargo must be put on board in such a way that her center of gravity will stay at the right level and directly in line above her center of buoyancy.

If all her cargo is put into her deep holds, her center of gravity will be too low. She will have more stability than is desirable, and her rolling will be heavy and abrupt.

If too much cargo is put on one side, she will list (tip to one side). If too much is put in her forward holds, she will be too low in the water at the bow. If too much is stowed aft, she will be too low at the stern. She will be out of trim (out of balance).

Sometimes a ship has to travel with little or no cargo aboard. Then she rides too high in the water. Her center of gravity is too high. She will roll too much, and too quickly, and in a bad storm she might even roll over. With too much freeboard exposed, her wind resistance is greater. Her propellers are not efficient, because they come out of the water.

To avoid all this she must add more weight to take the place of the missing cargo and thus lower her center of gravity again.

This extra weight is called ballast. A ship gets the extra weight she needs by filling her ballast tanks with seawater.

The ballast tanks are along the sides of the hull near the bottom. Most steel ships have double bottoms, for added safety, and the space between the inner and outer bottom can be used for ballast or for fuel tanks. Ships also often have ballast tanks in the forepeak (the

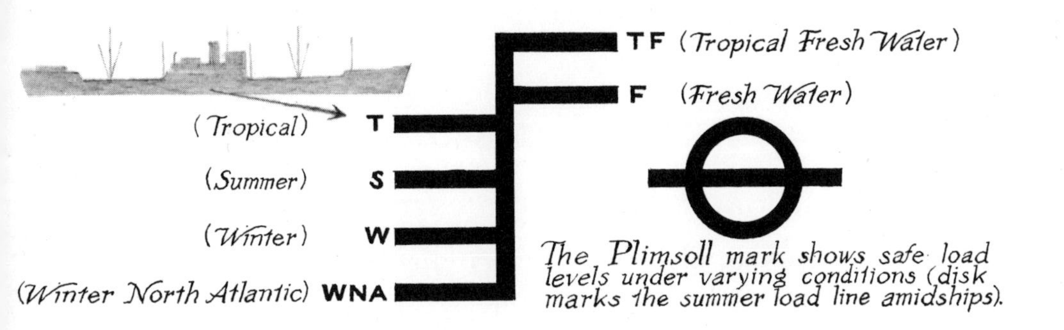

The Plimsoll mark shows safe load levels under varying conditions (disk marks the summer load line amidships).

extreme forward part inside the hull) and the afterpeak, to give them better balance fore and aft.

At her next port a lightly loaded ship may take on a large amount of cargo. Now she is so heavily loaded that she rides too low in the water. When this happens, water can be pumped out of the ballast tanks to lighten her.

An important safety feature on merchant ships is the Plimsoll mark painted on their sides. This mark prevents the overloading of a ship. It marks the limit of submergence allowed by law. When a ship sinks to this level in the water, no more weight can safely be added to her load.

Part of the weight a ship carries is her fuel oil. On long voyages she carries many tons of fuel, and as she uses it up she becomes lighter. Sometimes the weight of the fuel oil has to be replaced by taking more seawater into the ballast tanks.

In the days of sailing ships, bricks or bars of iron or heavy stones such as cobblestones were carried in the bottom of a ship as ballast. Today permanent ballast is used on many naval ships, small commercial ships, and sailboats, and all submarines. Large modern merchant ships, however, use only seawater for ballast.

In most cases, if a modern ship springs a leak or gets a hole knocked in her side, she will still remain afloat. This is because modern ships'

Stone-ballasting a fishing boat

hulls are divided up by bulkheads into many separate watertight compartments. For example, passenger ships are often eleven-compartment ships.

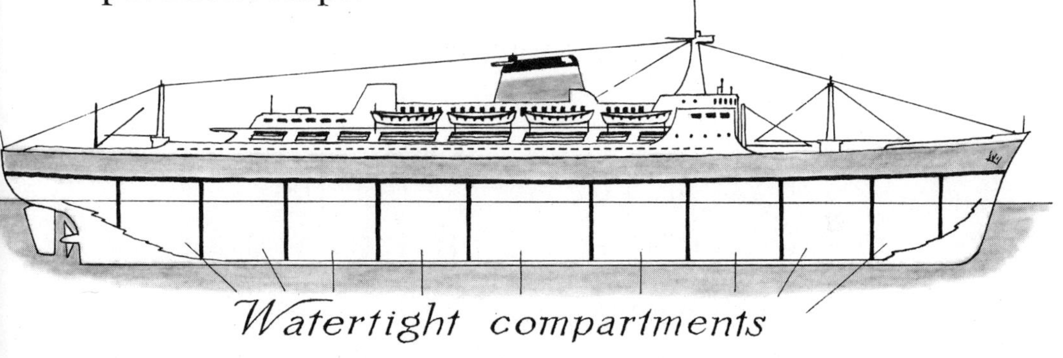

Watertight compartments

Even if a hole is made where a bulkhead is located, so that two compartments are flooded, most ships will remain afloat. The reason for this is that water seeks its own level. When the water in a flooded compartment reaches the level of the sea outside, it does not rise any higher. It cannot continue to rise, and therefore does not flood over the top of the compartment into the rest of the ship.

Damaged compartments will flood only to waterline

Not all ships are built to float. Some ships are built to *not* float. These ships are called submarines.

A submarine must be able both to float and sink. She must be able to dive under the water, stay for a long time, and then return to the surface.

A submarine must have a hull that is strong enough to resist great pressure, because the force with which water presses against anything increases enormously with each added foot of depth.

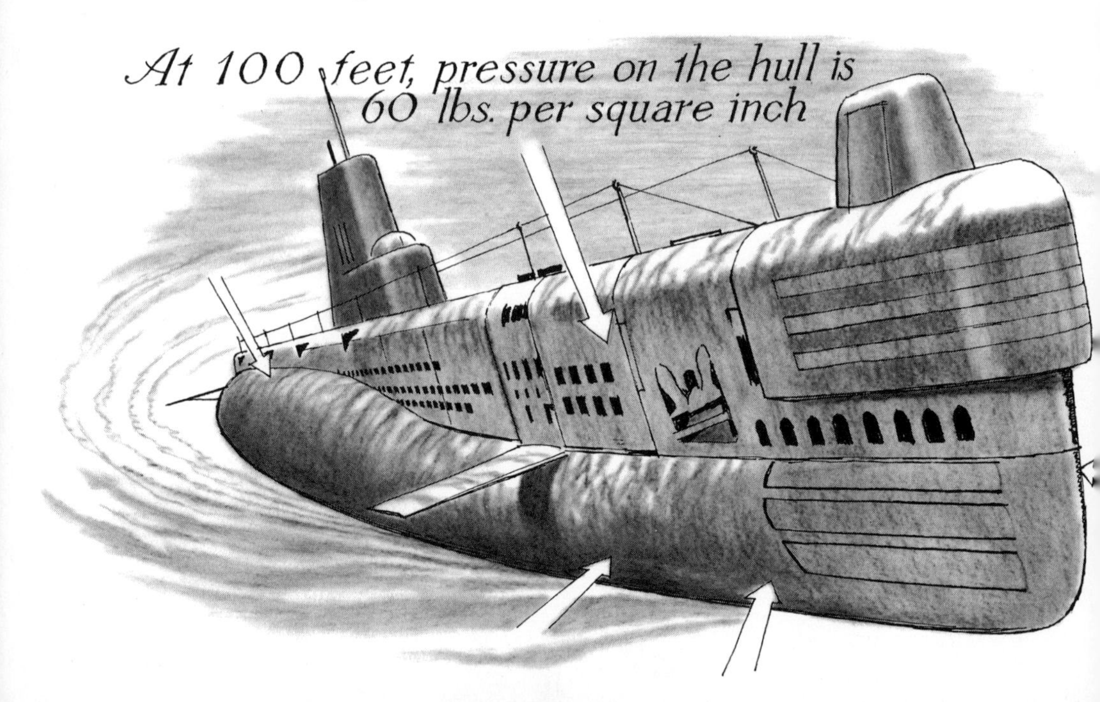

On the surface, water pressure equals atmospheric pressure, which is 14.7 pounds per square inch at sea level. For each extra foot of depth, the added pressure equals the weight of the water: 64 pounds per square foot for each extra foot of depth. At 33 feet, the pressure is 30 pounds per square inch. At 1,000 feet it is over 400 pounds per square inch.

Over most of their length, submarines have double hulls. The inner hull is the pressure hull. It is built of steel thick enough to resist great pressure. The outer hull is thin, because it does not have to resist the pressure of the water. The two hulls are the walls of her tanks, and when she is submerged the pressure on both sides of her outer hull is the same, because the tanks are filled with water.

When a submarine is on the surface, her tanks are filled with air. This gives her buoyancy enough to stay afloat.

When a submarine is ready to dive, her tanks are flooded with water. Seawater flows in through holes in the bottom of the tanks. The air inside is forced out by the water through valves in the top of the tanks. The weight of the water that takes the air's place gives the submarine a neutral weight, so that now it weighs the same as water.

In order to dive, a submarine has to use her propellers, diving planes, and stern planes. The planes are finlike plates which can be tilted at an angle, forcing the submarine down.

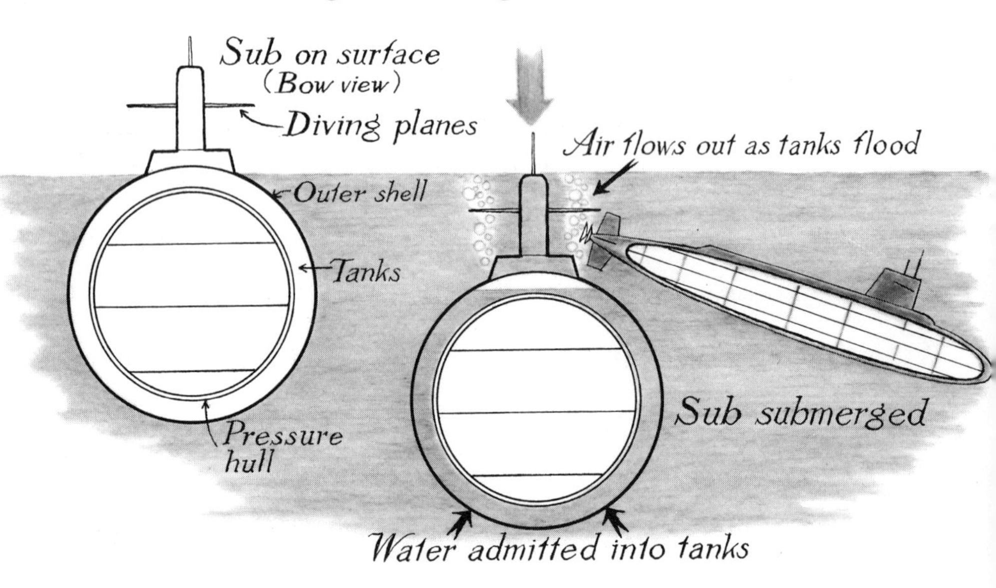

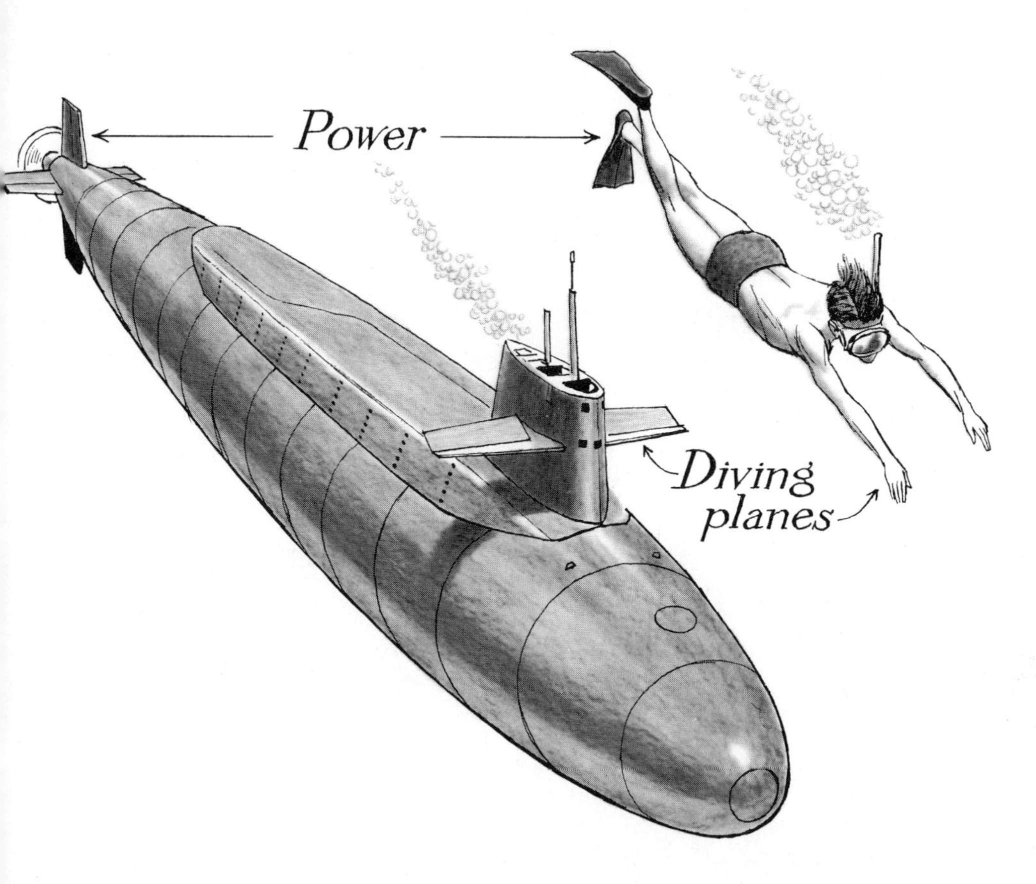

When a swimmer wants to go under water, he tilts his arms down for direction and kicks his feet for power. The less air he has in his lungs, the easier it is for him to sink. A submarine uses her planes and propellers in much the same way a swimmer uses his arms and legs.

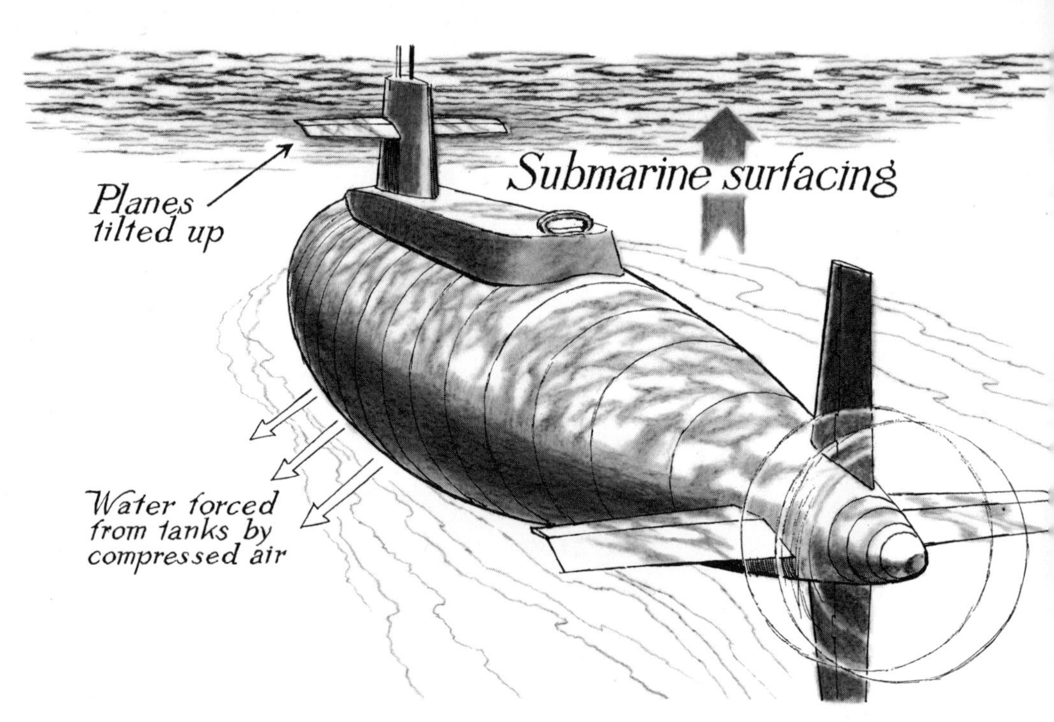

When a submarine is ready to come up again, compressed air is used to blow the seawater out of her tanks and take its place. Because it is compressed air, the pressure of the air is great enough to overcome the water pressure and force the seawater out of the tanks.

Now, instead of water, she again has air in her tanks, which increases her buoyancy. Her planes, which are now tilted upward, and her propellers drive her to the surface.

At present, a few thousand feet down is as deep as even our largest and strongest atomic submarines can safely go. At greater depths their pressure hulls would collapse inward.

To sink to the bottom of the ocean, men have to use special research submarines or bathyspheres or bathyscaphes. Bathyscaphes have two main parts. One is a large float. The other is a small ball-shaped cabin which usually has space for no more than two men.

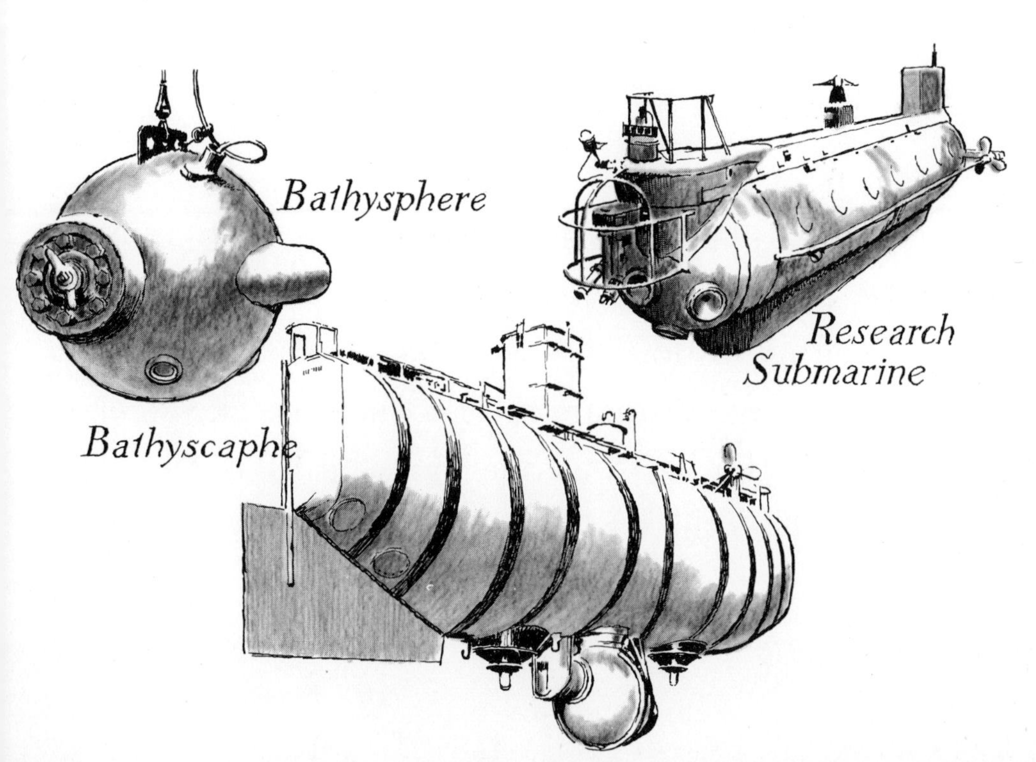

A bathyscaphe has reached the bottom in the deepest known part of the ocean, nearly seven miles down, where the pressure is eight tons on every square inch of surface. The steel hull of the bathyscaphe must be as much as five inches thick to resist this pressure.

The float, however, is made of thin steel plates. It is filled with gasoline. Gasoline is used because it weighs less than water. Its specific gravity is about 0.7. When the float is filled with gasoline, it can hold up the heavy cabin in the water.

The cabin is shaped like a ball because a ball can resist greater pressures than an object of any other shape (pressure pushes evenly against all parts of a ball's surface).

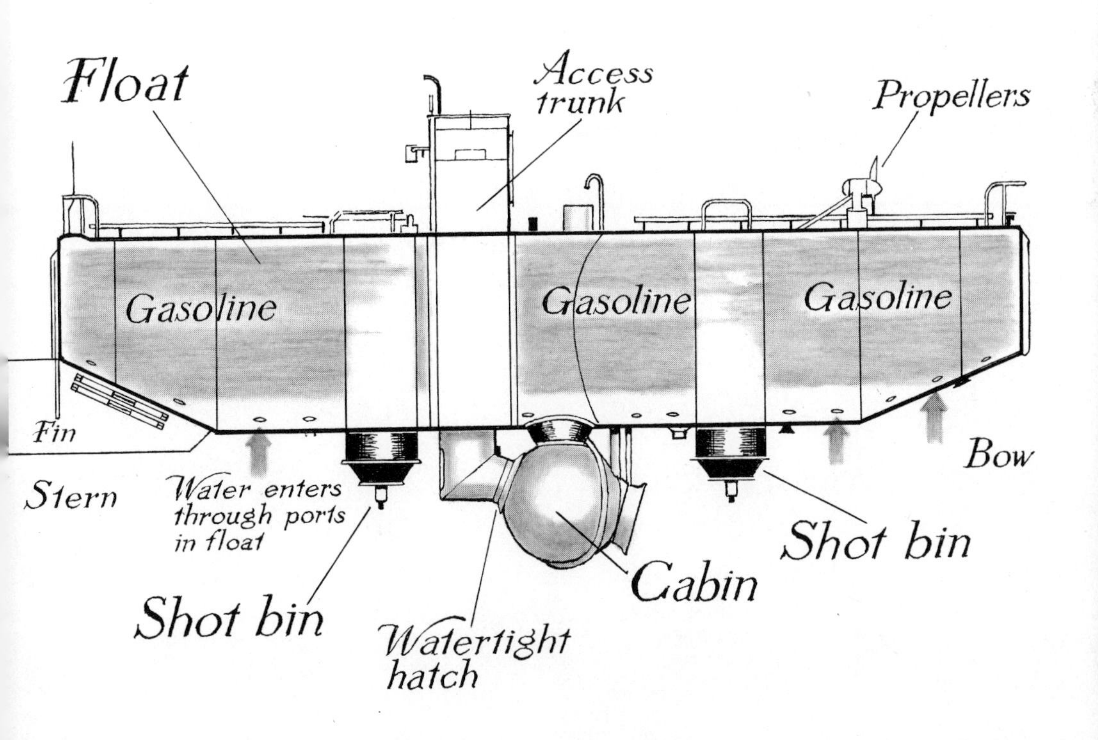

A bathyscaphe sinks because she carries extra weight on her sides in the form of bins filled with small iron pellets, or shot, that look much like BBs. This extra weight is just enough to pull the bathyscaphe under the surface of the water and allow her to sink.

The bottom of the float has holes in it that allow seawater to flow inside it. Since water and gasoline will not mix, the lighter gasoline floats on top of the water. As the bathyscaphe sinks deeper and deeper into the sea, the water presses harder and harder against the gasoline. In this way it forces the gasoline to press just as hard against the inside of the steel plates as the seawater is pressing against them from the outside.

Soon it is necessary to slow down the rate at which the bathyscaphe is sinking. This is done by releasing some of the iron shot. The pellets

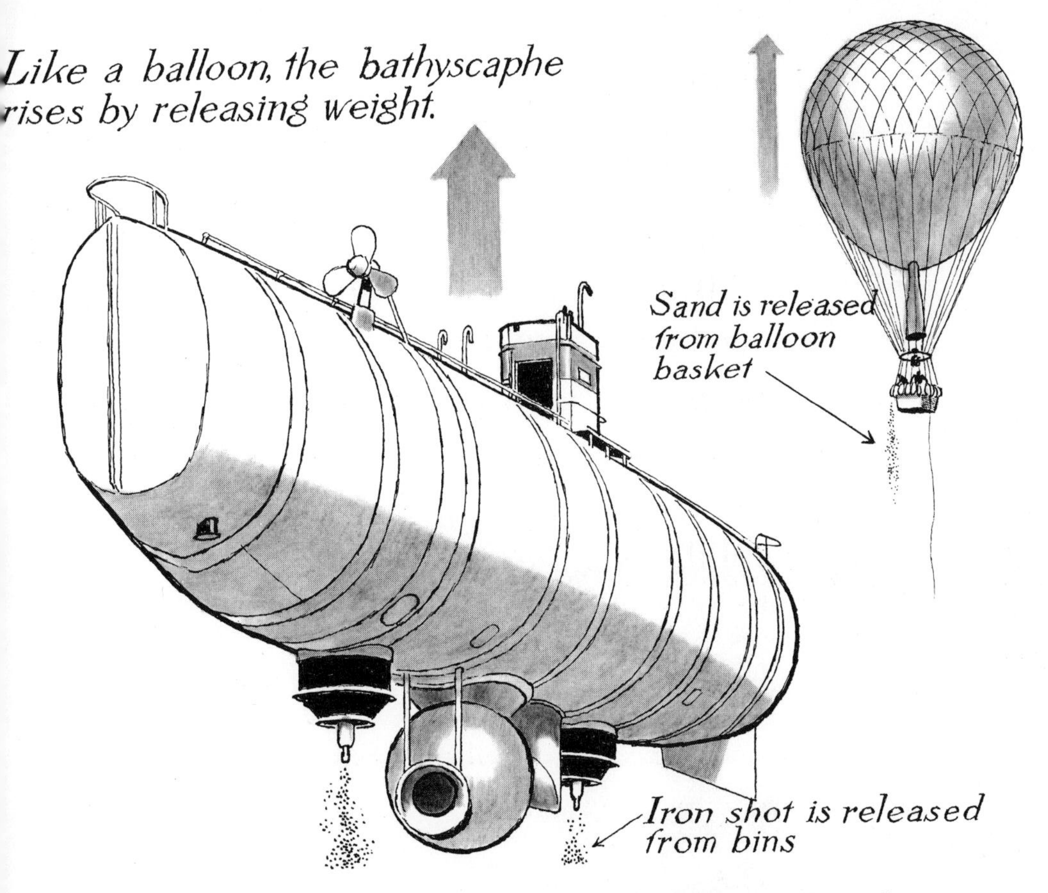

fall away into the water and thus make the bathyscaphe lighter.

When the pilot wants the bathyscaphe to return to the surface, he releases still more iron shot, until the bathyscaphe becomes light enough to start rising.

Boats have been made out of every possible material man could think of, from reeds, logs, birchbark, and canvas to aluminum, fiberglass, and plastics. Ships have even been made of reinforced concrete (concrete reinforced with steel rods). But no matter what boats are made of, the same basic rules apply to all.

What makes a boat float?

Buoyancy.

And what makes her stay afloat? Displacement, stability—and men who know how to handle her.

Index and Glossary

aft: at, close to, or toward the stern of a boat or ship. 10, 15, 17, 23, 25

afterpeak: the extreme rear part of the interior of a hull. 25

amidships: in or toward the middle part of a boat or ship. 15

ballast: heavy material carried in a ship to provide the desired draft and stability. 24–26

bathyscaphe: an underwater vehicle used for exploring the depths of the ocean. 33–34, 36–37

bathysphere: a ball-shaped diving apparatus lowered into the sea on a steel cable. 33

beam: a horizontal structural member, usually transverse, for supporting the decks of a boat or ship. 10

bow: the forward end of a boat or ship. 15, 23

bulkhead: wall-like partition inside a ship built to form watertight compartments, subdivide space, and strengthen the hull. 27

buoyancy: the supporting force exerted by a liquid upon a body wholly or partially immersed in it. The force is equal to the weight of the displaced liquid. 3–6, 13, 21, 29, 32, 38

buoyancy, center of: the point within a ship corresponding to the center of gravity of the volume of water displaced. 16, 18–21, 23

buoyancy, reserve: the additional buoyancy that would result if that part of the enclosed and watertight area of a ship that is above the waterline were immersed. 13–15 *camber:* the slight curve of a deck, arching upward from the sides toward the center. 15

capsize: to upset or overturn a ship. 16

cargo: the freight carried by a ship. 23–25

compartment: a space partitioned off by bulkheads. 27

compressed air: air under pressure greater than the atmosphere. 32

deck: a floorlike platform on a ship. 15, 22

density: mass per unit of volume. 6–7

displacement: the displacing in space of one mass by another; the weight or volume of fluid displaced by a floating or submerged object. It equals the weight of the vessel itself with whatever is on board. 3–7, 38

double bottom: the inner and outer bottoms which are part of the construction of most large ships. 24

equilibrium: a state of rest or balance due to the equal action of opposing forces. 19

forepeak: the extreme forward part of the interior of a hull. 25

forward: toward the bow of a ship. 10

frames: transverse, riblike members, or longitudinal members running between web frames to support and stiffen a hull; any of the skeleton structures forming the ribs or framework of a boat or ship. 10

freeboard: the portion of the side of a hull that is above the waterline. 13–15, 24

freighter: a ship used mainly for carrying cargo. 8

gravity: the pull of the earth's mass upon the mass of any object, otherwise called the object's weight. 3, 21

gravity, center of: the point through which the resultant of gravitational forces on an object passes. 16–24

gunwale: the upper edge of the side or bulwark of a boat or ship. 13

hold: the whole interior below decks, or strictly below the lower deck—where cargo is stored; any individual compartment of such cargo space. 23

hull: the hollow, lowermost portion of a boat or ship; the frame or body. 10–11, 13, 15, 18, 24–25, 27–29, 33

list: to lean to one side. 23

mass: the quantity of matter in anything. 3, 6

planes: horizontal control surfaces for submerging or elevating a submarine. 30–32

Plimsoll mark: a load-line mark painted on the sides of merchant ships, indicating the limit of submergence allowed by law. It was named after Samuel Plimsoll (1824–1898), the Englishman who brought about its adoption. 25

port: the left side of a boat or ship, facing forward. 10, 17

propeller: a device with two or more blades which turn in the water and make a ship move forward or backward. 24, 30–32

scupper: a drain hole at the edge of a deck, allowing water to flow overboard. 15

sheer: the fore-and-aft upward curve of the hull of a boat or ship at the main deck or bulwarks. 15

specific gravity: the ratio of the density of any substance to the density of some other substance (usually pure water) taken as standard. 8, 35

stability: the ability of a boat or ship to return to equilibrium after being disturbed by an outside force. 16, 23, 38

starboard: the right side of a boat or ship, facing forward. 10, 17, 20

stem: the forward part of a boat or ship. 10

stern: the after part of a boat or ship. 15, 20, 23

submarine: a ship that can be submerged and navigated under water. 26, 28–33 *submergence:* the state of being partly or wholly under water. 25

trim: the balance of a boat or ship in the fore and aft direction. 23

valve: any device for halting or controlling the flow of a liquid, gas, or other material through a pipe or passage. 30

volume: the amount of space that anything occupies. 3–4, 6–7, 9, 12

waterline: the part of the outside of a hull that is just at the water level. 11, 13, 20–21

water pressure: the exertion of force by water upon the surface of an object immersed in it. 29, 32

weight: the force exerted on any mass by the pull of gravity. 3–4, 6–7, 9–12, 14, 16–17, 19, 22, 24–26, 29–30, 36